ECONOMIC PERSPECTIVES ON MATERNAL AND CHILD HEALTHCARE

THE ECONOMIC VALUE OF HEALTHY MOTHERS AND CHILDREN

AMALA ANGEL ASHA M

MONIKANDA PRASAD G

*Dedicated to my beloved Parents
who are no longer with me in this world
but remain forever in my heart.*

Contents

Preface

The health and well-being of mothers and children are fundamental to the overall development and prosperity of any society. The economic dimensions of maternal and child healthcare, however, are often complex and multifaceted, intersecting with various aspects of public policy, healthcare delivery, and socioeconomic factors. This book, "Economic Perspectives on Maternal and Child Healthcare," seeks to unravel these complexities and provide a comprehensive understanding of how economic principles and policies influence maternal and child health outcomes.

The primary motivation for this book arises from the pressing need to address the disparities and inefficiencies that persist in maternal and child healthcare systems worldwide. Despite significant advancements in medical science and technology, many regions continue to experience high rates of maternal and child mortality, inadequate access to essential healthcare services, and substantial financial barriers to care. By examining these issues through an economic lens, we aim to identify sustainable solutions that can enhance healthcare delivery, improve health outcomes, and promote economic stability.

This book is structured to offer a detailed exploration of key economic concepts and their application to maternal and child healthcare. We begin by discussing the fundamental principles of health economics and their relevance to this field. Subsequent chapters delve into specific topics such as the economic impact of prenatal and postnatal care, the cost-effectiveness of various healthcare interventions, and the role of health insurance in improving access to care. We also address broader issues such as the economic consequences of maternal and child health disparities and the impact of public policies on healthcare delivery.

One of the unique features of this book is its interdisciplinary approach. We draw on insights from economics, public health, sociology, and policy analysis to provide a well-rounded perspective on the challenges and opportunities in maternal and child healthcare. By integrating these diverse viewpoints, we hope to offer readers a deeper understanding of the economic underpinnings of healthcare systems and the potential for innovative policy solutions.

This book is intended for a wide audience, including policymakers, healthcare professionals, researchers, and students. We aim to provide a valuable resource that not only enhances academic knowledge but also informs practical decision-making in the field of maternal and child healthcare. Our hope is that the insights and recommendations presented in this book will contribute to more equitable and efficient healthcare systems, ultimately improving the health and well-being of mothers and children around the world. In closing, we extend our heartfelt gratitude to the numerous individuals and organizations who have contributed to this book. Their expertise, support, and dedication have been instrumental in bringing this project to fruition. We also thank our readers for their interest in this important topic, and we encourage them to engage critically with the material and consider its implications for their own work and communities.

Acknowledgements

I express my heartfelt gratitude to all those who supported me in bringing this book to completion.

First, I thank my beloved parents, Michael Christopher and Sahaya Rathi, for nurturing in me a love for learning. Though they are no longer with me, their blessings and memories continue to inspire and guide me. I lovingly dedicate this book to them.

I am deeply grateful to my mentor, Dr. G. Monikanda Prasad, Assistant Professor and Head, Department of Economics, Manonmaniam Sundaranar University. His guidance, encouragement, and constant support have been a great source of strength throughout this journey.

I also wish to thank Prof. Dr. J. Sacratees, currently Registrar of Manonmaniam Sundaranar University. His encouragement and scholarly input, both as a senior faculty member in the Department of Economics and now as Registrar, have been of immense value to me.

My heartfelt thanks to my husband, Dr. K. Manoj, for being a constant source of encouragement and standing by me at every stage. I also thank my loving daughter, Rithanya Manoj, whose presence brought balance and happiness during this journey.

I appreciate the support of my colleagues, friends, and fellow researchers at Manonmaniam Sundaranar University for creating an encouraging academic environment.

To all my well-wishers—thank you for your kind words, encouragement, and belief in me.

— Amala Angel Asha M

Prologue

This comprehensive volume examines the vital intersection between economics, public health, and policy through the lens of maternal and child healthcare. By analyzing both theoretical frameworks and practical case studies, we demonstrate how investments in maternal and child health (MCH) yield substantial economic returns while advancing societal well-being and sustainable development.

The book's exploration begins with foundational economic concepts, establishing MCH as a crucial determinant of human capital formation. We present compelling evidence showing how healthy mothers and children form the bedrock of prosperous societies, with particular attention to the long-term economic benefits of reducing preventable mortality and morbidity. Our analysis includes rigorous assessments of cost-effective healthcare interventions that deliver exceptional returns on investment.

A significant portion of the work investigates healthcare system dynamics, identifying both barriers and innovative solutions to improve access and quality of care. We examine how infrastructure limitations, workforce shortages, and economic disparities create unequal health outcomes across populations. The discussion extends to policy formulation and implementation, featuring case studies of successful programs from diverse global contexts. These real-world examples illuminate the economic rationale for increased public and private sector investment in MCH.

The analysis further explores how social determinants - including poverty, education, and gender inequality - create health disparities with profound economic consequences. We present evidence linking early childhood health to adult productivity, demonstrating how malnutrition and inadequate prenatal care perpetuate intergenerational poverty cycles.

Looking forward, the book investigates emerging innovations in healthcare delivery, particularly the transformative potential of digital health technologies and data-driven approaches. We assess strategies for achieving Sustainable Development Goals related to MCH, emphasizing the need for integrated, multisectoral solutions.

Designed for economists, public health professionals, and policymakers, this volume serves as both a scholarly reference and practical guide. Students and researchers will find robust methodological frameworks, while practitioners gain actionable insights for program design and evaluation. The content balances academic rigor with accessible presentation, featuring:

- Comprehensive economic analysis of MCH investments
- Comparative policy studies from low-, middle-, and high-income countries
- Interdisciplinary approaches connecting health, education, and social protection
- Future-oriented strategies for health system strengthening

By systematically demonstrating the economic value of healthy mothers and children, this book makes an evidence-based case for prioritizing MCH in development agendas. Our findings show that strategic investments in this sector generate compounding benefits - producing healthier populations, more equitable societies, and more resilient economies. The conclusions provide policymakers with concrete recommendations to optimize resource allocation and maximize social returns on health investments.

This work ultimately reframes maternal and child health as not just a moral imperative, but as one of the most strategic investments nations can make in their future prosperity. It represents an essential resource for anyone committed to building sustainable health systems and achieving meaningful progress in global development.

CHAPTER ONE

Introduction

"Investing in maternal health is a wise economic choice. Healthy mothers raise healthy children who become productive members of society.

– Margaret Chan, Former Director-General, WHO"

Maternal and child health (MCH) is a foundational element of national development, directly influencing economic productivity, demographic transition, and human capital formation. Improvements in MCH contribute to healthier populations, reduced healthcare costs, and long-term economic growth. Conversely, poor maternal and child health can lead to lifelong consequences including chronic illness, underdevelopment, and intergenerational poverty.

The economic implications of MCH are increasingly recognized by policymakers, healthcare providers, and researchers. Maternal health affects not only the well-being of mothers but also the survival and development of their children. Investment in MCH yields high social and economic returns, making it an essential component of public policy and health planning.

This chapter introduces the core concepts underpinning MCH from an economic lens. It outlines the rationale for this book, which integrates economic analysis with public health perspectives to understand and improve maternal and child outcomes. It also details the structure of the book, which progresses from theoretical foundations to practical case studies, offering a comprehensive view of the topic.

Globally, there have been significant improvements in MCH indicators over the past few decades, yet disparities persist. In India, while programs like the National Health Mission and Janani Suraksha Yojana have improved access and outcomes, challenges remain in rural areas, marginalized communities, and regions with weak infrastructure. Understanding the economic consequences of these health outcomes is key to designing effective policies.

1.1 Importance of MCH in National Development

Healthy mothers and children form the basis of a productive society. Improved MCH contributes to labor force participation, educational attainment, and economic productivity. Neglecting MCH can result in lost human potential and economic stagnation.

1.2 Health as a Component of Human Capital

Human capital refers to the attributes—such as education, health, and skills—that contribute to an individual's economic productivity. MCH is the earliest form of human capital investment. Poor health in infancy or during pregnancy can reduce cognitive ability, learning outcomes, and lifetime earnings.

1.3 Economic Rationale for Investment in MCH

Spending on MCH is not just a social imperative but an economic strategy. For every dollar invested in maternal and child health, multiple dollars are saved in future health costs and productivity losses. Preventive care, early interventions, and comprehensive health services lead to long-term economic benefits.

1.4 Structure and Approach of the Book:

This book is structured into 17 chapters:

- Chapters 1 and 2 introduce the economic foundations of MCH.
- Chapters 3 to 6 analyze trends, determinants, and expenditure patterns.
- Chapters 7 to 14 cover policy interventions, implementation issues, technological innovations, and inclusive strategies.
- Chapters 15 to 17 offer case studies, identify challenges, and provide policy recommendations.

1.5 Key Definitions and Indicators:

- **Maternal Mortality Ratio (MMR):** Number of maternal deaths per 100,000 live births.
- **Infant Mortality Rate (IMR):** Number of infant deaths per 1,000 live births.
- **Under-five Mortality Rate (U5MR):** Deaths of children under five years of age per 1,000 live births.
- **Skilled Birth Attendance:** Percentage of births attended by trained health personnel.
- **Antenatal Care (ANC) Coverage:** Proportion of women receiving at least four antenatal visits.

This introductory chapter sets the stage for a multidisciplinary exploration of maternal and child health. It aims to highlight the intersection of economics and health and to build a compelling case for prioritizing MCH in policy, planning, and public investment.

Theoretical Perspectives on Maternal and Child Health

The study of maternal and child health (MCH) has evolved through various theoretical lenses that draw upon disciplines such as public health, sociology, economics, anthropology, and gender studies. The integration of these theoretical frameworks helps to understand the complex interplay of biological, social, economic, and political factors influencing the health outcomes of women and children.

2.1 Biomedical Model

The biomedical model focuses primarily on the biological and physiological aspects of maternal and child health. It emphasizes disease pathology, diagnosis, and treatment, typically addressing the health of individuals rather than considering broader determinants. Although this model has significantly contributed to the reduction of maternal and child mortality through advances in medical technology and institutional delivery, it falls short in addressing the social and economic root causes of health disparities (Engel, 1977).

2.2 Social Determinants of Health Framework

This framework recognizes that health outcomes are shaped by a range of social, economic, and environmental factors. According to the World Health Organization (2008), determinants such as education, income, occupation, gender, and geographic location influence access to health services and overall well-being. For instance, a mother's education level strongly correlates with improved infant immunization rates and reduced neonatal mortality (Gwatkin et al., 2007).

2.3 Life Course Theory

The life course approach posits that maternal and child health is shaped by biological and social exposures that occur across a person's lifetime. Health outcomes are not the result of isolated events but the cumulative impact of risk and protective factors over time. For example, poor nutrition during a mother's childhood may increase her risk of complications during pregnancy, which in turn can affect her child's future development (Halfon & Hochstein, 2002).

2.4 Feminist and Gender Theories

Feminist perspectives examine how patriarchal structures and gender inequalities affect maternal and child health. These theories argue that systemic biases in healthcare delivery and policy often marginalize women's voices and experiences. Access to reproductive healthcare, maternal autonomy in decision-making, and societal attitudes toward women's health are critical dimensions in this framework (Sen & Östlin, 2008).

2.5 Economic Theories of Health Behavior

Economic theories, such as the Grossman model of health capital (Grossman, 1972), view health as both a consumption and investment good. Health is seen as a product of household decisions constrained by income, education, and time. Mothers invest in prenatal care, child nutrition, and immunization based on perceived benefits and opportunity costs. This framework is valuable for evaluating cost-effectiveness and designing incentives in public health programs (Becker, 1993).

2.6 Ecological Systems Theory

Proposed by Bronfenbrenner (1979), this theory considers the multiple levels of influence on a child's development—from the immediate family to the broader socio-economic and cultural environment. It is particularly useful for understanding how neighborhood, policy, and institutional factors affect child health outcomes.

2.7 Human Rights-Based Approach

This framework asserts that health is a fundamental human right and stresses accountability and equity. Governments have a duty to ensure that all women and children enjoy the highest attainable standard of health without discrimination. This approach underlies many international conventions, such as the Convention on the Elimination of All Forms of Discrimination Against Women (CEDAW) and the Convention on the Rights of the Child (UNICEF, 2001).

2.8 Conclusion

Theoretical perspectives on maternal and child health offer distinct but complementary insights. While biomedical advances save lives, social, gendered, economic, and ecological lenses reveal the deeper causes of inequity and offer pathways for holistic interventions. A multi-theoretical approach is essential for designing effective, inclusive, and sustainable MCH policies and programs.

CHAPTER THREE

Trends in Maternal and Child Health in India

India, as a developing nation with a large and diverse population, has witnessed substantial changes in maternal and child health (MCH) over the past few decades. Improvements in medical infrastructure, policy interventions, community health programs, and international collaboration have significantly influenced the health indicators of women and children. However, despite progress, challenges such as regional disparities, undernutrition, and unequal access to care persist.

3.1 Historical Overview

Post-independence India struggled with high maternal and infant mortality rates due to poor sanitation, limited health services, and widespread poverty. The introduction of the National Family Health Survey (NFHS) in the early 1990s provided robust data to track health indicators and shape policies (International Institute for Population Sciences [IIPS] & Macro International, 1995). Subsequent surveys have been instrumental in analyzing progress.

3.2 Maternal Mortality Trends

India's maternal mortality ratio (MMR) has decreased significantly, from 556 deaths per 100,000 live births in 1990 to 97 in 2020 (Sample Registration System [SRS], 2022). This decline is attributed to increased institutional deliveries, better emergency obstetric care, and antenatal services. Yet, disparities remain across states. Kerala and Tamil Nadu report low MMRs, while Uttar Pradesh and Bihar continue to face higher risks due to inadequate health infrastructure and socioeconomic constraints (Registrar General of India, 2022).

3.3 Child Mortality and Morbidity

The under-five mortality rate in India declined from 125 per 1,000 live births in 1990 to 32 in 2022 (UNICEF, 2023). Neonatal mortality has also seen consistent reductions. Public health initiatives like the Universal Immunization Programme (UIP), Integrated Child Development Services (ICDS), and Mission Indradhanush have been critical in addressing child mortality (Ministry of Health and Family Welfare, 2021).

3.4 Nutrition and Stunting

Malnutrition remains a major concern, especially among children under five. According to NFHS-5 (2019–21), about 35.5% of children under five years are stunted, and 32.1% are underweight (IIPS & ICF, 2021). Anaemia prevalence is high among pregnant women and adolescent girls. Programs like POSHAN Abhiyaan aim to tackle these issues through multi-sectoral interventions.

3.5 Institutional Deliveries and Skilled Birth Attendance

There has been a significant rise in institutional deliveries—from 39% in 2005–06 (NFHS-3) to 88.6% in 2019–21 (NFHS-5). The Janani Suraksha Yojana (JSY), a conditional cash transfer program under the National Health Mission (NHM), incentivized institutional births and helped bridge urban-rural gaps (Lim et al., 2010).

3.6 Urban-Rural and Socioeconomic Disparities

Despite improvements, vast disparities persist. Urban areas report better maternal and child health outcomes compared to rural regions. Marginalized groups—such as Scheduled Castes, Scheduled Tribes, and minorities—often face systemic barriers in accessing care. Social determinants such as female literacy, income levels, and cultural practices influence outcomes significantly (Bhargava & Tiwari, 2015).

3.7 Impact of COVID-19

The COVID-19 pandemic disrupted essential maternal and child health services, particularly in rural and underserved regions. Antenatal checkups, immunization drives, and nutrition programs were temporarily halted or scaled down, affecting coverage and outcomes (UNFPA India, 2021). However, digital health platforms and teleconsultations emerged as alternative modes of care delivery.

3.8 Government and International Interventions

Various national programs and global collaborations have played a pivotal role in improving MCH. Notable initiatives include:

- National Health Mission (NHM)
- Pradhan Mantri Matru Vandana Yojana (PMMVY)
- POSHAN Abhiyaan
- WHO, UNICEF, and World Bank partnerships for technical and financial support

These initiatives collectively aim to improve access, affordability, and quality of healthcare for mothers and children.

3.9 Conclusion

India has made commendable progress in reducing maternal and child mortality and improving health service delivery. However, sustained investments in health systems, targeted interventions for vulnerable populations, and efforts to address social determinants are vital for achieving universal maternal and child health.

CHAPTER FOUR

Determinants of Maternal and Child Health Outcomes

Maternal and child health (MCH) is profoundly shaped by economic factors at the individual, household, community, and national levels. Income, employment, access to financial resources, and health expenditures directly influence access to healthcare, nutrition, and sanitation—all critical for ensuring maternal and child well-being. This chapter explores these economic determinants in detail, highlighting how financial inequality contributes to disparities in health outcomes.

4.1 Household Income and Poverty

One of the most significant determinants of MCH is household income. Low-income families often struggle to afford nutritious food, hygienic living conditions, and quality healthcare services. Poverty increases the risk of maternal mortality due to delayed or non-existent antenatal care and complications during childbirth. Similarly, children in poor households are more likely to be undernourished and face higher risks of infections and mortality (World Bank, 2019). Poverty also limits education, particularly for girls, reducing future health awareness and healthcare-seeking behavior.

4.2 Employment and Women's Economic Participation

Women's employment and control over resources play a critical role in improving maternal and child health. Economically empowered women are more likely to utilize maternal health services, invest in their children's nutrition and education, and make informed decisions regarding fertility and family planning (Duflo, 2012). However, informal sector employment, which lacks maternity benefits and health insurance, often limits these benefits. Gender wage gaps and occupational segregation further marginalize women economically.

4.3 Health Expenditure and Out-of-Pocket Costs

High out-of-pocket expenditure (OOPE) is a major barrier to accessing healthcare in India. According to the National Health Accounts (2022), over 48% of total health spending in India is borne by households. In rural areas, where public health infrastructure is often inadequate, families rely on private providers, incurring high costs. The burden of OOPE for delivery, postnatal care, and child treatment can plunge low-income households into debt or discourage them from seeking timely care (Berman et al., 2010).

4.4 Insurance Coverage and Financial Risk Protection

Health insurance is a vital mechanism to protect households from catastrophic health expenditures. Government-sponsored schemes such as the Pradhan Mantri Jan Arogya Yojana (PM-JAY) offer financial risk protection to poor families. However, coverage gaps, inadequate awareness, and bureaucratic hurdles limit the effectiveness of these programs. Increasing enrollment in insurance schemes and improving claim processes can significantly enhance MCH outcomes by reducing financial barriers (Karan et al., 2017).

4.5 Public Health Financing and Budget Allocation

Government spending on health as a percentage of GDP remains low in India, limiting infrastructure development and human resource availability in public facilities. While the National Health Policy (2017) aims to increase public health expenditure to 2.5% of GDP, implementation remains slow. States with higher public health spending, such as Kerala and Tamil Nadu, have achieved better maternal and child health indicators compared to low-expenditure states (NITI Aayog, 2020).

4.6 Economic Inequality and Social Exclusion

Economic inequality, often compounded by caste, religion, and gender, creates structural barriers to health access. Marginalized communities face discrimination in service provision and limited participation in health governance. Programs must therefore be equity-focused and designed to overcome the entrenched social determinants of poor health outcomes.

4.7 Cost-Benefit Analysis of Investing in MCH

Investments in maternal and child health yield substantial economic returns. Improved maternal health reduces productivity losses and healthcare costs. Healthy children are more likely to achieve educational milestones and grow into productive adults. According to a WHO study, every dollar spent on MCH generates a nine-fold return through enhanced productivity and reduced disease burden (WHO, 2015).

4.8 Conditional Cash Transfer Programs

Conditional cash transfers (CCTs), such as the Janani Suraksha Yojana (JSY) and Pradhan Mantri Matru Vandana Yojana (PMMVY), provide financial incentives to encourage institutional deliveries and antenatal care. These programs have shown positive impacts, especially among economically disadvantaged groups, by reducing barriers to accessing healthcare services (Lim et al., 2010).

4.9 Microfinance and Women's Health

Access to microcredit has empowered women economically and socially, enabling them to spend on health services and nutrition. Self-help groups (SHGs) that link financial services with health education have been successful in enhancing awareness and improving maternal and child health practices at the grassroots level (Saha, 2017).

4.10 Economic Policy and Health Equity

Macroeconomic policies, such as taxation and social protection, influence resource distribution and equity in healthcare. Pro-poor policies that prioritize health in national budgets, implement progressive taxation, and expand social safety nets can reduce disparities and enhance MCH outcomes. Effective policy implementation requires intersectoral coordination and community participation.

4.11 Conclusion

Economic factors significantly impact maternal and child health outcomes. Income, employment, health financing, and public policy shape access to essential services and influence health behaviors. Addressing economic determinants through inclusive growth, financial risk protection, and targeted investments in healthcare infrastructure is essential to achieving sustainable improvements in maternal and child health.

CHAPTER FIVE

Health Infrastructure and Access to Maternal and Child Healthcare

An effective healthcare infrastructure forms the backbone of any health system and plays a decisive role in ensuring safe pregnancies and healthy child development. The availability, accessibility, affordability, and quality of healthcare facilities determine maternal and child health (MCH) outcomes in both urban and rural areas. This chapter delves into the role of health infrastructure in shaping MCH, including the availability of skilled professionals, functioning facilities, geographic accessibility, and the role of public versus private systems.

5.1 Overview of Health Infrastructure in India

India's health system is structured into three tiers: primary, secondary, and tertiary care. At the primary level, sub-centres and primary health centres (PHCs) provide basic services including antenatal and postnatal care. Secondary and tertiary facilities offer specialist services and emergency obstetric care. However, disparities in infrastructure across states, rural-urban areas, and regions continue to affect maternal and child health indicators (National Health Systems Resource Centre, 2020).

5.2 Availability of Healthcare Facilities

Access to adequate healthcare facilities is a prerequisite for safe deliveries and proper neonatal care. Many rural areas still face a lack of functioning health centres, labor rooms, and equipment. Shortfalls in PHCs and community health centres (CHCs), along with outdated facilities, hinder the provision of essential maternal health services (Ministry of Health and Family Welfare, 2021).

5.3 Human Resource Gaps

The shortage of skilled health personnel—including doctors, nurses, and midwives—limits the reach of maternal and child healthcare services. Skilled birth attendance is a critical determinant of maternal survival. The World Health Organization (WHO) recommends a minimum density of 4.45 health workers per 1,000 population, a target many Indian states fall short of (WHO, 2016). Strengthening human resources through training, deployment, and retention is essential.

5.4 Geographic and Socioeconomic Barriers

Physical distance to health centres, especially in tribal and hilly regions, poses a significant barrier. Poor road connectivity and lack of transportation options deter women from seeking timely antenatal and delivery care. Socioeconomic barriers such as caste, class, and gender further compound these challenges, making healthcare inaccessible for marginalized communities (Baru et al., 2010).

5.5 Urban-Rural Disparities

Urban areas, especially metropolitan cities, often enjoy better-equipped hospitals, higher health worker density, and greater choice of services. In contrast, rural regions face poor infrastructure, absenteeism of health staff, and irregular supply chains. This urban-rural divide is evident in higher maternal mortality ratios (MMR) and infant mortality rates (IMR) in rural India (NITI Aayog, 2020).

5.6 Role of Private Healthcare Providers

The private sector plays a dominant role in healthcare provision in India, especially in urban areas. While it contributes to expanding access, the high cost of services, variable quality, and profit motives often restrict its role in equitable maternal care. Many families turn to private providers due to inadequate public services, but without insurance or subsidies, this imposes financial burdens (Patel et al., 2015).

5.7 Functioning of Public Health Programs

Government programs such as the Reproductive, Maternal, Newborn, Child, and Adolescent Health (RMNCH+A) strategy aim to improve MCH outcomes by strengthening health systems and outreach. Programs like Janani Shishu Suraksha Karyakram (JSSK) provide free services for deliveries and newborn care in public hospitals. Evaluations suggest these have increased institutional births, but challenges persist in service delivery and quality (UNICEF, 2019).

5.8 Quality of Care and Service Delivery

Quality of care goes beyond the availability of infrastructure—it involves respectful treatment, clinical competence, cleanliness, and follow-up care. Poor patient-provider interactions, long waiting times, and lack of privacy discourage utilization of maternal services. Strengthening service quality through training, monitoring, and community feedback mechanisms is essential for trust and sustained utilization (Bohren et al., 2015).

5.9 Innovations in Health Infrastructure

Technological innovations like telemedicine, mobile health clinics, and digital health records are expanding access to MCH services in remote areas. Mobile health (mHealth) applications help monitor pregnancies and deliver health information. While promising, these innovations require digital literacy, infrastructure, and integration with existing health systems (Singh et al., 2018).

5.10 Policy Recommendations

Improving MCH infrastructure requires a multi-pronged approach: increasing budget allocations, upgrading facilities, ensuring drug supply, addressing staff shortages, and engaging communities. Decentralized planning and district-level monitoring can help tailor interventions. Public-private partnerships, when regulated, can complement public efforts in underserved areas.

CHAPTER SIX

Maternal Nutrition and Its Economic Implications

Maternal nutrition plays a fundamental role in determining the health outcomes of both mothers and their children. Adequate nutrition during pregnancy ensures proper fetal growth, reduces complications during childbirth, and fosters long-term developmental outcomes for children. Poor maternal nutrition is not only a public health concern but also an economic issue, as it affects productivity, healthcare costs, and intergenerational human capital. This chapter explores the multi-dimensional impacts of maternal nutrition, with emphasis on its economic ramifications, policy interventions, and the challenges in ensuring nutritional security for women in India.

6.1 The Importance of Maternal Nutrition

Maternal nutrition encompasses the dietary intake and nutritional status of women during preconception, pregnancy, and lactation. It directly influences the birth weight, immune function, and cognitive development of the newborn. The World Health Organization (WHO, 2020) identifies maternal malnutrition as a key factor in maternal mortality and infant morbidity. Micronutrient deficiencies, particularly iron, folate, calcium, and iodine, are prevalent in Indian women and contribute to anemia, preterm birth, and low birth weight.

6.2 Prevalence and Patterns of Malnutrition Among Women in India

India faces a dual burden of undernutrition and overnutrition among women of reproductive age. According to the National Family Health Survey-5 (NFHS-5, 2021), 57% of women aged 15–49 are anemic, with higher prevalence in rural areas and among lower-income groups. Stunting and wasting in children are closely associated with maternal nutritional status. Inadequate dietary diversity, cultural food taboos, and poverty exacerbate the nutritional deprivation of pregnant women.

6.3 Economic Consequences of Maternal Malnutrition

Malnutrition contributes to a cycle of poverty and poor health outcomes. Maternal undernutrition can lead to complications such as obstructed labor, hemorrhage, and increased susceptibility to infections, raising healthcare expenditures. Low birth weight children may have developmental delays, lower educational attainment, and reduced earning potential. The World Bank (2019) estimates that countries can lose up to 3% of GDP due to productivity losses from malnutrition. Addressing maternal nutrition thus yields high returns in terms of economic growth and human development.

6.4 Direct and Indirect Costs

The direct costs of poor maternal nutrition include increased spending on healthcare services, extended hospital stays, and higher rates of maternal and infant mortality. Indirect costs arise from reduced workforce participation, absenteeism, and lower productivity among malnourished mothers. Poor cognitive development in malnourished children, often linked to inadequate maternal diet, affects educational outcomes and future earning capacity (Victora et al., 2008).

6.5 Determinants of Maternal Nutrition

A range of factors determines maternal nutritional status. These include:

- **Socioeconomic status:** Women from lower-income households often have limited access to nutritious food.
- **Education:** Maternal education correlates with better dietary choices and health-seeking behavior.
- **Cultural practices:** Traditional beliefs and food taboos during pregnancy can lead to nutrient deficiencies.
- **Healthcare access:** Regular antenatal care (ANC) visits provide nutritional counseling and supplements.
- **Food security:** Seasonal food shortages and inflation affect household dietary intake.

6.6 Government Programs and Interventions

India has implemented several schemes to address maternal nutrition. The Integrated Child Development Services (ICDS) provides supplementary nutrition to pregnant and lactating women. The Pradhan Mantri Matru Vandana Yojana (PMMVY) offers conditional cash transfers for institutional deliveries and nutrition. The POSHAN Abhiyaan, launched in 2018, aims to reduce stunting, undernutrition, and anemia through convergence of multiple ministries (Ministry of Women and Child Development, 2021).

6.7 Challenges in Implementation

Despite well-designed policies, implementation gaps persist. Issues include inadequate infrastructure, shortage of frontline workers, low community participation, and inconsistent monitoring. Corruption and leakages in food distribution systems hinder effectiveness. Moreover, awareness among beneficiaries regarding the importance of nutrition remains low (Bhawra et al., 2020).

6.8 Role of NGOs and Community-Based Approaches

Non-governmental organizations play a vital role in delivering nutrition services, especially in underserved areas. Community-based strategies, such as women's self-help groups and peer educators, have shown success in promoting dietary awareness and supplement uptake. Local production of fortified foods and kitchen gardens are innovative ways to improve access to nutritious food at the household level (Ghosh, 2022).

6.9 Nutrition During Adolescent and Preconception Periods

Addressing nutritional needs prior to pregnancy is equally important. Adolescent girls must receive adequate nutrition to ensure healthy pregnancies in the future. Early marriage and repeated pregnancies worsen nutritional status. Policies must therefore adopt a life-course approach, promoting nutrition from adolescence through motherhood (UNICEF, 2018).

6.10 Policy Recommendations

Improving maternal nutrition requires multisectoral action:

- Strengthen food-based interventions and expand fortified food distribution.
- Promote nutrition education through mass media and community health workers.
- Enhance monitoring and evaluation mechanisms in existing programs.
- Increase budgetary allocations to nutrition-specific and nutrition-sensitive interventions.
- Encourage private sector partnerships in food fortification and delivery.

6.11 Conclusion

Maternal nutrition is a critical component of public health and economic development. Addressing nutritional deficiencies not only improves maternal and child health outcomes but also enhances workforce productivity and reduces healthcare costs. A sustained focus on implementation, community engagement, and intersectoral coordination is key to achieving national nutrition goals.

CHAPTER SEVEN

Child Nutrition and Human Capital Development

Child nutrition is a critical foundation for human capital formation and long-term economic growth. Nutritional status in early childhood significantly influences cognitive development, educational attainment, and future labor market outcomes. Inadequate nutrition during the formative years can cause irreversible damage to physical and mental development, leading to lower productivity and earnings in adulthood. This chapter explores the multidimensional effects of child nutrition on economic development, with a focus on the Indian context.

7.1 The Significance of Early Childhood Nutrition

The first 1,000 days of a child's life—from conception to two years—represent a critical window for nutritional intervention. Proper nutrition during this period ensures optimal brain development, growth, and immune function. Undernutrition, particularly stunting and wasting, during these years has lasting effects on school performance and adult productivity (Black et al., 2013).

7.2 Nutritional Indicators in India

Despite economic progress, India continues to grapple with high levels of child malnutrition. According to the NFHS-5 (2021), 35.5% of children under five years are stunted, 19.3% are wasted, and 32.1% are underweight. These statistics reflect persistent food insecurity, inadequate maternal nutrition, poor sanitation, and limited access to healthcare.

7.3 Consequences of Child Malnutrition

Child malnutrition imposes a heavy economic burden. Stunted children are more likely to drop out of school, perform poorly academically, and have lower earning potential. Malnutrition-related morbidity increases healthcare costs and reduces parental productivity. At the macroeconomic level, malnutrition can result in a 2–3% loss in GDP annually (Hoddinott et al., 2013).

7.4 Education and Nutrition Nexus

There is a strong bidirectional relationship between education and nutrition. Malnourished children face learning difficulties, reduced attention spans, and higher absenteeism. Conversely, parental education—especially maternal education—correlates with better child feeding practices and health-seeking behavior. School feeding programs have been effective in improving both nutritional and educational outcomes (Drèze & Goyal, 2003).

7.5 Social Determinants of Child Nutrition

Several interlinked factors influence child nutrition:

- **Poverty:** Limits access to adequate and nutritious food.
- **Maternal health:** Poor maternal nutrition leads to low birth weight and developmental issues.
- **Gender disparities:** Girls are more likely to suffer from malnutrition due to cultural biases.
- **Water and sanitation:** Open defecation and unsafe water sources increase risk of diarrheal diseases.

7.6 National Programs and Interventions

India has implemented a number of programs to improve child nutrition:

- **Integrated Child Development Services (ICDS):** Provides supplementary nutrition, preschool education, and health services.
- **Mid-Day Meal Scheme:** Offers free meals in schools to improve nutrition and enrollment.
- **POSHAN Abhiyaan:** Aims to reduce stunting, anemia, and low birth weight through a multi-sectoral approach (Ministry of Women and Child Development, 2021).

7.7 Implementation Challenges

Despite wide coverage, these programs face multiple challenges:

- Inadequate infrastructure and trained personnel.
- Leakage of resources and poor quality of food.
- Inconsistent monitoring and evaluation.
- Lack of community engagement and ownership.

7.8 Role of Private Sector and Civil Society

Partnerships with private organizations and NGOs can enhance service delivery and innovation. Fortification of food products, behavioral change campaigns, and technology-based monitoring systems can complement government efforts. Corporate social responsibility (CSR) initiatives can be aligned with nutrition goals to improve outcomes in underserved regions (Bhawra et al., 2020).

7.9 Global Experiences and Lessons for India

Countries like Brazil and Bangladesh have successfully reduced child malnutrition through integrated programs focusing on maternal education, conditional cash transfers, and robust monitoring. India can adapt similar strategies by promoting intersectoral convergence and strengthening decentralized governance structures (UNICEF, 2018).

7.10 Policy Recommendations

To combat child malnutrition effectively, the following policy measures are recommended:

- Scale up nutrition-sensitive interventions targeting early childhood.
- Improve coordination between health, education, and social welfare departments.
- Strengthen capacity-building of frontline workers and increase community participation.
- Integrate nutrition indicators into school assessments.
- Expand social safety nets and food security programs.

7.11 Conclusion

Child nutrition is foundational to a nation's economic success. By investing in the health and nutrition of children, countries can break the intergenerational cycle of poverty and build a more productive workforce. Holistic, data-driven, and inclusive policies are essential for translating nutrition interventions into tangible developmental gains.

CHAPTER EIGHT

Health Financing for Maternal and Child Healthcare

Health financing plays a critical role in shaping the accessibility, affordability, and quality of maternal and child healthcare services. An efficient and equitable health financing system ensures that no individual is deprived of essential care due to financial barriers. This chapter delves into the mechanisms of health financing, its importance in maternal and child health (MCH), existing models in India, challenges, global best practices, and recommendations for creating a robust financial architecture to support MCH.

8.1 Understanding Health Financing in the Context of MCH

Health financing involves the mobilization, allocation, and utilization of financial resources to deliver health services. For maternal and child health, financing must cover prenatal care, skilled birth attendance, postnatal care, immunizations, nutrition, and emergency services. These interventions have long-term economic and social benefits (WHO, 2010).

8.2 Importance of Public Financing in MCH

Public financing ensures risk pooling, equity, and access to services irrespective of income. In low- and middle-income countries, out-of-pocket (OOP) expenses form a significant portion of healthcare spending, pushing many into poverty (Xu et al., 2003). Public spending on maternal and child health is an investment in human capital and can reduce long-term costs associated with poor health outcomes.

8.3 Health Financing Landscape in India

India's healthcare system is characterized by low public health expenditure and high OOP spending. As of 2020, public health spending stood at around 1.3% of GDP, among the lowest globally (National Health Accounts, 2021). Several schemes have been introduced to address this gap:

- **Janani Suraksha Yojana (JSY):** A conditional cash transfer scheme to promote institutional deliveries.
- **Janani Shishu Suraksha Karyakram (JSSK):** Provides free maternity and neonatal services in public facilities.
- **Ayushman Bharat – Pradhan Mantri Jan Arogya Yojana (PMJAY):** Offers financial protection for secondary and tertiary care to over 50 crore beneficiaries.

8.4 High Health Costs and Family Burden

High OOP expenditure remains a concern in India, particularly for maternal and child health services. According to NSSO (2018), nearly 60% of maternity care expenses are borne out-of-pocket. Catastrophic health spending can deter families from seeking timely care, leading to increased maternal and infant mortality.

8.5 Role of Health Insurance in MCH

Health insurance schemes, both public and private, aim to mitigate the financial burden of healthcare. While schemes like PMJAY have expanded coverage, gaps remain in outpatient and preventive services, which are crucial for MCH. Moreover, awareness, enrollment, and utilization of insurance schemes remain low in rural areas (Karan et al., 2017).

8.6 Financing for Preventive vs. Curative Services

Preventive healthcare—such as immunizations, antenatal check-ups, and nutritional programs—is often underfunded despite its cost-effectiveness. A shift from curative to preventive spending is vital to improve maternal and child health outcomes and reduce the disease burden in the long term

(Jamison et al., 2013).

8.7 Donor and NGO Contributions

International donors and NGOs have historically contributed to maternal and child health through funding, technical assistance, and implementation support. Organizations like UNICEF, WHO, and the World Bank have provided critical resources for improving immunization, nutrition, and maternal care services. However, donor dependence is unsustainable, necessitating increased domestic resource mobilization.

8.8 Financing Equity and Marginalized Groups

Equity in financing ensures that vulnerable groups—such as the poor, women in rural areas, tribal populations, and minorities—receive adequate healthcare. Targeted subsidies, community health financing, and decentralized budget allocations are essential strategies to address disparities (Rao et al., 2011).

8.9 Global Best Practices in Health Financing for MCH

Countries like Thailand, Sri Lanka, and Rwanda have demonstrated success through universal health coverage and strategic purchasing. Thailand's Universal Coverage Scheme, for example, significantly reduced maternal mortality through comprehensive service packages and capitation payments (Tangcharoensathien et al., 2018).

8.10 Policy Recommendations

To strengthen health financing for maternal and child health in India:

- Increase public health expenditure to at least 2.5% of GDP.
- Expand financial protection mechanisms for outpatient and preventive services.
- Strengthen monitoring and accountability in public health spending.
- Promote public-private partnerships to leverage additional resources.
- Enhance community participation in budgeting and resource allocation.

8.11 Conclusion

Adequate and equitable financing is the bedrock of an effective maternal and child health system. By aligning financial strategies with public health goals, India can ensure that every mother and child has access to essential health services without suffering financial hardship. Progressive investments in MCH will yield high economic and social returns, fostering inclusive and sustainable development.

CHAPTER NINE

Government Policies and Programs for Maternal and Child Health

Government policies and programs are instrumental in shaping health outcomes for mothers and children. They provide the legal, financial, and institutional framework necessary for delivering healthcare services across urban and rural regions. This chapter outlines the evolution of maternal and child health (MCH) policies in India, major national programs, challenges in implementation, and suggestions for future policy directions.

9.1 Historical Overview of MCH Policies in India

India has a long history of public health policy development. The post-independence era witnessed the introduction of the Community Development Program (1952) and the National Family Planning Program (1952), which laid the foundation for later MCH interventions. The Maternal and Child Health Program was formally launched in 1953 to provide immunization, nutrition, and antenatal care services (Bajpai & Goyal, 2004).

In 1975, the Integrated Child Development Services (ICDS) program was launched, focusing on child nutrition, immunization, and health education. The 1980s and 1990s saw the introduction of the Universal Immunization Programme and Child Survival and Safe Motherhood Programme, which emphasized basic health services for mothers and children.

9.2 National Health Mission (NHM)

Launched in 2005, the NHM amalgamated the National Rural Health Mission (NRHM) and the National Urban Health Mission (NUHM). Its goals include reducing infant and maternal mortality, improving access to quality healthcare, and ensuring effective implementation of health programs.

The NHM supports decentralized planning, community participation, and improved infrastructure through initiatives like:

- Accredited Social Health Activists (ASHAs)
- Village Health Sanitation and Nutrition Committees (VHSNCs)
- Rogi Kalyan Samitis

NHM has significantly improved access to antenatal care, institutional deliveries, and immunization (MoHFW, 2021).

9.3 Janani Suraksha Yojana (JSY)

Introduced in 2005, JSY is a conditional cash transfer program under NHM. It incentivizes institutional deliveries among poor pregnant women, especially in rural areas. JSY has led to a marked increase in institutional deliveries, particularly in states with high maternal mortality ratios (Lim et al., 2010).

9.4 Janani Shishu Suraksha Karyakram (JSSK)

Launched in 2011, JSSK aims to eliminate out-of-pocket expenses for pregnant women and sick newborns by offering free services such as delivery, cesarean section, diagnostics, blood transfusions, and transport. It complements JSY and enhances financial risk protection for maternal and child care (MoHFW, 2013).

9.5 Reproductive, Maternal, Newborn, Child and Adolescent Health (RMNCH+A)

The RMNCH+A strategy, introduced in 2013, provides a continuum of care across all stages of life. It integrates reproductive, maternal, newborn, child, and adolescent health services and emphasizes inter-sectoral convergence. Key interventions include antenatal care, skilled birth attendance, essential newborn care, and adolescent health education (UNICEF, 2014).

9.6 POSHAN Abhiyaan (National Nutrition Mission)

Launched in 2018, POSHAN Abhiyaan aims to reduce stunting, undernutrition, anemia, and low birth weight among children and women. It integrates multiple ministries and leverages technology for real-time monitoring. The program empowers Anganwadi workers and promotes behavioral change through community-based events and Jan Andolan campaigns (NITI Aayog, 2020).

9.7 Pradhan Mantri Matru Vandana Yojana (PMMVY)

PMMVY is a maternity benefit program that provides cash incentives to pregnant and lactating women for their first child. The scheme promotes health-seeking behavior by encouraging registration, antenatal check-ups, and breastfeeding. It also complements other schemes like JSY and JSSK (MoWCD, 2018).

9.8 Challenges in Implementation

Despite numerous programs, challenges persist:

- Fragmentation and overlap between schemes
- Inadequate health infrastructure and human resources
- Poor monitoring and accountability mechanisms
- Low awareness among beneficiaries
- Gender and social disparities

Moreover, centralized planning often fails to address local health needs, and rural-urban divides continue to impact service delivery (Berman et al., 2010).

9.9 Policy Recommendations

To improve the effectiveness of MCH policies and programs:

- Strengthen inter-sectoral coordination and convergence
- Increase investments in primary healthcare infrastructure
- Improve data systems for monitoring and evaluation
- Empower frontline health workers with training and resources
- Ensure community participation and decentralized planning

9.10 Conclusion

India's commitment to improving maternal and child health is evident in its extensive policy framework and range of programs. However, effective implementation and sustained political will are essential to translate policies into health outcomes. By addressing systemic challenges and adopting an inclusive, community-based approach, India can ensure equitable access to quality healthcare for mothers and children.

CHAPTER TEN

Public-Private Partnerships in Maternal and Child Health

Public-Private Partnerships (PPPs) have emerged as a powerful strategy to bridge the gaps in the delivery of healthcare services, particularly in developing countries like India. These collaborations combine the strengths of the public sector—such as outreach, infrastructure, and policy support—with the innovation, efficiency, and resources of the private sector. In the domain of maternal and child health (MCH), PPPs play a critical role in improving access, quality, and affordability of care.

10.1 Concept and Importance of PPPs in Healthcare

PPPs refer to cooperative arrangements between public authorities and private sector entities aimed at delivering public services or infrastructure. In healthcare, this could involve financing, construction, management, or operation of facilities and services. For MCH, PPPs help fill the void left by public system limitations such as shortage of skilled personnel, inadequate infrastructure, and logistical barriers (Rao et al., 2012).

These partnerships are crucial because:

- They expand the reach of essential services to underserved areas.
- Enhance the quality of care through technology and expertise.
- Promote innovation in service delivery models.
- Improve efficiency and accountability in healthcare operations.

10.2 Models of PPPs in MCH

PPPs in maternal and child health operate through various models:

- **Contracting out services**: The government contracts private entities to manage and operate public facilities or deliver specific services, like diagnostic labs or ambulance services.
- **Franchising models**: Private providers operate under a common brand or protocol, maintaining service standards while expanding access (e.g., Marie Stopes or Janani clinics).
- **Social marketing**: Private companies are engaged to promote and distribute health products like contraceptives and ORS at subsidized rates.
- **Collaborative training and capacity building**: Public and private institutions jointly develop and implement training programs for healthcare personnel.

10.3 Case Studies of Successful PPPs in India

India has witnessed several successful PPP initiatives in MCH:

- **Chiranjeevi Yojana (Gujarat)**: Aimed at reducing maternal mortality, this scheme contracted private obstetricians to provide free delivery services to poor women. It resulted in a significant increase in institutional deliveries and reduction in maternal deaths (Bhat et al., 2009).
- **Vatsalya Scheme (Uttar Pradesh)**: Encouraged private gynecologists to deliver services to Below Poverty Line (BPL) women. Though initially promising, sustainability and quality control became concerns.
- **Mobile Medical Units (MMUs)**: Implemented across many states, these units, often operated by private agencies, bring antenatal and child health services to remote areas.

10.4 Opportunities and Benefits of PPPs in MCH

The main advantages of leveraging PPPs in MCH include:

- **Improved service delivery**: PPPs help scale up essential services such as institutional delivery, immunization, and neonatal care.
- **Increased investment**: Private sector participation introduces capital and technological innovation.
- **Reduced burden on public resources**: Shared responsibilities help the government allocate resources efficiently.
- **Enhanced accountability and performance**: Defined contracts and measurable outcomes improve quality assurance.

10.5 Challenges in Implementing PPPs

Despite their benefits, PPPs face several challenges in MCH:

- **Regulatory hurdles**: Ambiguities in legal frameworks and lack of standardization often delay implementation.
- **Quality assurance**: Monitoring and enforcing quality standards across diverse providers is complex.
- **Equity issues**: PPPs may favor profit-driven motives over equitable access.
- **Sustainability concerns**: Dependence on external funding or changes in political will can disrupt service continuity.

10.6 Best Practices for Effective PPPs

For PPPs to be effective in MCH, the following best practices should be adopted:

- **Clear policy frameworks**: Transparent guidelines on contract design, implementation, and performance evaluation.
- **Robust monitoring mechanisms**: Strong data systems to track health outcomes and service delivery.

- **Community engagement**: Involving local stakeholders to ensure cultural relevance and accountability.
- **Capacity building**: Joint training initiatives to enhance public and private sector capabilities.

10.7 Future Directions for PPPs in MCH

Going forward, the focus should be on developing scalable and replicable PPP models that prioritize maternal and child health equity. Innovations such as telemedicine, digital health records, and AI-based diagnostics can be integrated through public-private collaboration. Additionally, policy coherence and sustained funding are essential for long-term success.

10.8 Conclusion

Public-Private Partnerships offer a promising pathway to strengthen maternal and child healthcare systems in India. While they are not a panacea for all health system challenges, when carefully designed and implemented, PPPs can significantly enhance access, efficiency, and quality of care. A balanced approach that aligns public goals with private capabilities, supported by robust governance, can ensure lasting impact on maternal and child health outcomes.

CHAPTER ELEVEN

Innovations and Technology in Maternal and Child Healthcare

In recent decades, technological innovation has dramatically transformed healthcare delivery worldwide. Maternal and Child Health (MCH), a critical aspect of public health, has greatly benefited from advances in digital health, medical devices, data analytics, and communication systems. In a country like India, where geographic, socio-economic, and infrastructural barriers affect access to care, the application of modern technologies presents a promising path toward improving maternal and child outcomes.

11.1 Role of Technology in MCH

Technology enhances MCH services by ensuring timely interventions, improving diagnosis and treatment, facilitating health worker training, and streamlining program monitoring. Mobile health (mHealth) applications, telemedicine, electronic health records (EHRs), and artificial intelligence (AI)-powered tools have all contributed to better quality, efficiency, and equity in care.

Some of the core areas of impact include:

- **Remote access to care** through teleconsultations and digital diagnostics.
- **Real-time monitoring of pregnancies and high-risk cases.**
- **Improved patient education** through mobile apps and SMS-based services.

- **Health worker empowerment** via e-learning tools and decision-support systems.
- **Efficient data collection and analysis** for planning and policy-making.

11.2 Mobile Health (mHealth) Applications

India has seen a rapid rise in mHealth initiatives designed to educate, monitor, and support pregnant women and new mothers. Government-supported applications like **Kilkari**, which sends weekly voice messages to pregnant women, and **Mobile Academy**, which trains frontline workers, have shown significant improvements in awareness and service utilization (Agarwal et al., 2015).

Private innovations like **BabyChakra**, **PregBuddy**, and **Maatritva** offer appointment tracking, nutritional tips, and access to peer support networks. These platforms bridge the information gap and foster timely health-seeking behavior.

11.3 Telemedicine and Remote Consultations

Telemedicine bridges geographic divides, connecting rural mothers with specialists in urban centers. Government schemes like **eSanjeevani** enable doctor-to-doctor and doctor-to-patient consultations across state-run facilities. This helps in:

- Managing high-risk pregnancies remotely.
- Providing pediatric care in underserved regions.
- Reducing travel costs and delays in receiving care.

11.4 AI and Predictive Analytics

Artificial Intelligence and machine learning are being increasingly used in MCH to analyze large datasets and identify at-risk mothers and children. Predictive algorithms help in:

- Early identification of complications like preeclampsia or gestational diabetes.

- Customized treatment plans based on individual profiles.
- Prioritization of limited healthcare resources (Jain & Raza, 2020).

11.5 Wearables and Point-of-Care Devices

Innovations in wearable technology and low-cost diagnostic devices have made real-time monitoring of maternal and infant health easier. Examples include:

- Wearable fetal heart rate monitors.
- Bluetooth-enabled blood pressure cuffs.
- Portable hemoglobin analyzers for anemia detection.

Such tools are especially valuable in community settings where laboratory infrastructure is weak.

11.6 Digital Health Records and Data Systems

Digitization of health records enhances continuity of care, reduces duplication, and allows health workers to track outcomes. Programs like **Reproductive and Child Health (RCH) Portal** and **Health Management Information System (HMIS)** support data-driven decision-making at policy and program levels.

Challenges remain, however, such as ensuring data privacy, interoperability between systems, and the digital literacy of users.

11.7 Innovations in Health Communication and Training

Frontline health workers, especially ASHAs and ANMs, benefit from digital platforms that offer:

- Interactive training modules.
- Visual content on maternal nutrition and neonatal care.
- Real-time chat support and updates from supervisors.

Innovations like **TeCHO+** in Gujarat and **CommCare** in several states exemplify such training and monitoring tools.

11.8 Limitations and Barriers

Despite their potential, technological interventions in MCH face obstacles:

- **Infrastructure gaps**: Poor internet connectivity in remote areas.
- **Digital divide**: Low smartphone access among rural women.
- **User resistance**: Cultural reluctance to adopt tech-mediated care.
- **Cost and scalability**: High costs limit widespread deployment of some technologies.

Addressing these challenges requires public investment, community involvement, and partnerships with tech innovators.

11.9 Future Directions

To further strengthen MCH outcomes through technology:

- Expand universal mobile access and internet connectivity.
- Integrate AI-powered decision support into primary care.
- Encourage local startups to develop culturally sensitive tools.
- Establish data governance frameworks to ensure privacy and equity.

11.10 Conclusion

Technology is not a replacement but a powerful supplement to traditional maternal and child healthcare systems. When harnessed appropriately, innovations can democratize access, personalize care, and ultimately reduce maternal and child morbidity and mortality. Policymakers must focus on inclusive, equitable, and context-specific digital solutions to realize the full benefits of technology in MCH.

CHAPTER TWELVE

Improving Maternal Health through Better Nutrition

Maternal nutrition plays a pivotal role in determining pregnancy outcomes, birth weight, and long-term health trajectories of both mother and child. In India, maternal undernutrition and anemia remain critical challenges, especially among low-income and marginalized communities. These nutritional deficiencies contribute significantly to maternal morbidity, neonatal mortality, and intergenerational cycles of poor health.

12.1 Importance of Maternal Nutrition

During pregnancy, a woman's body undergoes profound physiological changes that increase nutritional requirements. Adequate intake of macronutrients—carbohydrates, proteins, and fats—as well as micronutrients—iron, folate, calcium, and iodine—is vital to:

- Support fetal growth and development.
- Prevent pregnancy complications.
- Improve maternal immunity and energy levels.
- Reduce risks of preterm birth and low birth weight.

The nutritional status before conception also matters, as undernourished women are at higher risk of adverse outcomes (Black et al., 2013).

12.2 Prevalence of Undernutrition and Anemia

According to the National Family Health Survey (NFHS-5), over 50% of pregnant women in India are anemic, and nearly 20% have a low body mass index (BMI). The prevalence is higher in rural areas, among adolescent mothers, and in states like Bihar, Jharkhand, and Madhya Pradesh (IIPS, 2021).

Factors contributing to this include:

- Poor dietary diversity.
- Inadequate meal frequency.
- Cultural food taboos.
- Teenage pregnancies.
- Heavy workloads and low autonomy in household decision-making.

12.3 Government Initiatives and Supplementation Programs

India has implemented several programs aimed at improving maternal nutrition:

- **POSHAN Abhiyaan**: Launched in 2018, it seeks to reduce stunting, anemia, and low birth weight through convergence and real-time monitoring.
- **Iron and Folic Acid (IFA) Supplementation**: Under the Anemia Mukt Bharat (AMB) initiative, pregnant women receive 180 iron-folic acid tablets during pregnancy.
- **Integrated Child Development Services (ICDS)**: Provides take-home rations and nutrition counseling through Anganwadi Centers.
- **Janani Suraksha Yojana (JSY)** and **Pradhan Mantri Matru Vandana Yojana (PMMVY)**: Offer conditional cash transfers to incentivize antenatal care and nutrition.

However, program coverage and compliance remain inconsistent.

12.4 Dietary Patterns and Local Food Solutions

Improving maternal nutrition requires promoting dietary diversity and locally available foods. Nutrient-rich food groups include:

- Pulses, legumes, and dairy for protein.
- Green leafy vegetables for iron and calcium.
- Citrus fruits for Vitamin C.
- Fortified cereals and iodized salt.

Community-level interventions such as kitchen gardens, women's self-help groups, and nutrition awareness sessions can increase access and uptake of healthy foods (Ruel & Alderman, 2013).

12.5 Role of Frontline Workers

Accredited Social Health Activists (ASHAs), Auxiliary Nurse Midwives (ANMs), and Anganwadi Workers (AWWs) play a vital role in:

- Identifying and tracking high-risk pregnancies.
- Providing IFA tablets and counseling on diet.
- Referring severely undernourished women to health facilities.
- Conducting community-based cooking demonstrations and nutrition days.

Capacity building of these workers through digital tools and refresher training is essential for effective service delivery.

12.6 Addressing Adolescent Nutrition

Adolescent girls form a critical group in breaking the intergenerational cycle of malnutrition. Early marriage and childbearing compound nutritional deficits. Programs like the **Weekly Iron and Folic Acid Supplementation (WIFS)** and school-based nutrition education aim to improve adolescent health and delay pregnancy.

12.7 Challenges in Implementation

Despite multiple programs, challenges include:

- Irregular supply of supplements and fortified foods.
- Poor monitoring and follow-up.
- Lack of individualized counseling.
- Limited male involvement in maternal nutrition.

Innovative approaches, such as digital tracking of supplement distribution and nutrition-sensitive agriculture, can address some of these gaps.

12.8 Integrating Nutrition into Health Systems

Maternal nutrition should be embedded within antenatal care through:

- Routine screening for anemia and underweight.
- Counseling during ANC visits.
- Linkages with food security schemes like Public Distribution System (PDS).
- Multi-sectoral collaboration between health, agriculture, education, and women's welfare departments.

12.9 Future Priorities

- Strengthening last-mile delivery of supplements.
- Empowering women with information on food choices.
- Enhancing data use for planning and monitoring.
- Ensuring community ownership of nutrition programs.

12.10 Conclusion

Addressing maternal undernutrition and anemia is essential to improving maternal and child health outcomes. A life-cycle approach that includes adolescent girls, pregnant women, and lactating mothers is vital. Sustainable improvement requires community engagement, robust systems, and convergence of nutrition with health and social development initiatives.

CHAPTER THIRTEEN

Health Education and Awareness: Empowering Mothers through Information

Health education is a cornerstone of maternal and child health initiatives, playing a crucial role in enabling women to make informed decisions regarding their health and the well-being of their children. Empowering mothers with accurate and timely information can significantly improve the uptake of health services, nutrition practices, hygiene behaviors, and disease prevention strategies.

13.1 Importance of Health Education in Maternal Care

Educating women, particularly during pregnancy and the postpartum period, helps them understand:

- The importance of regular antenatal check-ups.
- Nutritional needs during and after pregnancy.
- Early signs of complications and when to seek care.
- Benefits of institutional delivery and skilled birth attendance.
- Breastfeeding practices and immunization schedules.

Women who are informed are more likely to adhere to medical advice, seek timely healthcare, and adopt behaviors that enhance the health of both themselves and their children (WHO, 2016).

13.2 Sources of Health Information

Women receive health information through multiple sources, including:

- **Healthcare providers**: Doctors, nurses, midwives, and frontline workers.
- **Community health workers**: ASHAs, ANMs, and Anganwadi Workers provide doorstep counseling.
- **Mass media**: Television, radio, and newspapers.
- **Digital platforms**: Mobile phones, SMS services, and apps like Kilkari and mMitra.
- **Community groups**: Self-help groups and women's collectives.

Each of these sources plays a unique role in shaping health knowledge and practices.

13.3 Government Campaigns and Initiatives

Several government initiatives have been launched to spread health awareness among mothers:

- **Janani Shishu Suraksha Karyakram (JSSK)**: Promotes free maternity services and encourages institutional deliveries.
- **Kilkari**: A mobile voice messaging service delivering weekly audio messages to pregnant women and new mothers.
- **Saathiya Resource Kit**: A peer educator model under the Rashtriya Kishor Swasthya Karyakram (RKSK).
- **Mother and Child Protection Card**: Provides key information about pregnancy, childbirth, immunization, and nutrition.

These tools are designed to be culturally appropriate, easy to understand, and accessible even in low-literacy settings (UNICEF, 2019).

13.4 Role of Frontline Workers in Health Education

Frontline workers are the primary interface between the health system and the community. Their roles include:

- Conducting home visits for counseling.
- Organizing community meetings and mothers' groups.
- Demonstrating infant feeding techniques.
- Distributing educational materials.
- Encouraging antenatal care visits and institutional deliveries.

Effective communication skills and cultural sensitivity are essential for building trust and overcoming barriers such as myths, stigma, and low literacy.

13.5 Digital Innovations in Health Communication

With increasing mobile phone penetration, digital tools are being leveraged to provide health education:

- **Kilkari**: Sends weekly voice messages in regional languages.
- **Mobile Academy**: Trains ASHAs through audio-based learning modules.
- **mMitra**: Offers personalized voice calls to pregnant women and new mothers.
- **WhatsApp groups**: Used for sharing information and addressing queries.

These platforms allow timely, scalable, and cost-effective dissemination of health messages (Gopichandran et al., 2017).

13.6 Addressing Health Misinformation and Myths

Misinformation, cultural myths, and superstitions often undermine maternal and child health. Health education must address:

- Myths around food restrictions during pregnancy.
- Misconceptions about colostrum.

- Beliefs regarding delivery methods and postnatal care.
- Rumors about vaccines causing infertility or illness.

Correcting these through respectful dialogue, evidence-based messages, and community engagement is vital for improving health behaviors.

13.7 Literacy and Gender Barriers

Low literacy and gender inequality affect women's access to health information. Strategies to overcome these include:

- Use of pictorial materials and storytelling.
- Engaging male partners and family elders.
- Organizing health camps and street plays.
- Promoting girls' education as a long-term investment.

Inclusive approaches ensure that no woman is left behind in accessing vital information.

13.8 Measuring the Impact of Health Education

The effectiveness of health education can be measured through:

- Knowledge, Attitudes, and Practice (KAP) surveys.
- Health indicators like antenatal care visits and institutional deliveries.
- Feedback from mothers and community members.
- Changes in breastfeeding rates and immunization coverage.

Data-driven evaluation helps refine programs and scale successful models.

13.9 Future Priorities

- Strengthening training for health educators.
- Expanding mobile-based learning.
- Localizing messages for tribal and remote populations.
- Fostering community leadership in health promotion.
- Linking health education with empowerment and livelihood initiatives.

13.10 Conclusion

Health education is a powerful tool for empowering mothers and improving maternal and child health outcomes. Through multi-channel communication, community involvement, and a focus on behavioral change, informed women can lead healthier lives and contribute to healthier families. Integrating education into every aspect of health service delivery ensures long-lasting impact and sustainable development.

CHAPTER FOURTEEN

Community Role in Mother and Child Healthcare

Community participation is a cornerstone of sustainable health systems, especially in the realm of maternal and child health (MCH). When communities are involved in the design, implementation, and evaluation of health programs, outcomes tend to improve, reflecting better alignment with local needs and greater ownership of health initiatives. Community involvement fosters transparency, accountability, and a sense of responsibility, enabling long-lasting behavioral changes and stronger support structures for women and children.

14.1 Understanding Community Participation

Community participation in MCH refers to the active involvement of individuals, families, local leaders, and community-based organizations in decision-making and action related to health service delivery. Participation can take several forms:

- Attending health education sessions.
- Engaging in planning and monitoring local health programs.
- Supporting vulnerable families during pregnancy and childbirth.
- Advocating for better facilities and services.

This participatory approach not only enhances the effectiveness of health interventions but also ensures that cultural, social, and economic factors influencing health are taken into account (Rifkin, 2009).

14.2 Historical Context in India

India's commitment to community-based health care began with the Alma Ata Declaration of 1978, which emphasized primary health care and community involvement. This was further solidified by the National Rural Health Mission (NRHM) in 2005, which introduced:

- Village Health, Sanitation, and Nutrition Committees (VHSNCs).
- Accredited Social Health Activists (ASHAs) as community mobilizers.
- Community monitoring mechanisms for public health services.

These initiatives aimed to decentralize health governance and bring decision-making closer to the people (MoHFW, 2018).

14.3 Structures Enabling Participation

Several institutional structures support community engagement in maternal and child health programs:

- **VHSNCs:** Comprising local leaders, ASHAs, and women's representatives, they monitor local health services, promote sanitation, and ensure community participation.
- **Rogi Kalyan Samitis (RKS)**: Manage the affairs of public health institutions and include elected members of local government.
- **Self-help Groups (SHGs)**: Often engage in health-related discussions and economic empowerment, increasing women's confidence and autonomy.
- **Health and Nutrition Days**: Provide platforms for health education, ANC checkups, and community interaction.

These platforms facilitate dialogue between health providers and the community and encourage problem-solving based on local realities.

14.4 Empowering Women as Change Agents

Women's involvement in community health decisions has shown to increase the relevance and responsiveness of health programs. Empowered women, when given leadership roles:

- Advocate for improved services and infrastructure.
- Encourage peers to seek care and adopt healthy practices.
- Facilitate early detection of maternal and child health risks.
- Demand accountability from service providers.

The process of empowerment, through participation, builds agency and solidarity among women, which is crucial for improving MCH outcomes (Bhutta et al., 2010).

14.5 Challenges to Effective Participation

Despite the potential, several barriers hinder meaningful community involvement:

- Power dynamics and gender inequality.
- Lack of training and awareness among community members.
- Inadequate funding and institutional support.
- Tokenistic participation, where community voices are not taken seriously.

Addressing these challenges requires long-term capacity building, inclusive representation, and a shift in the mindset of health administrators and providers.

14.6 Community Monitoring and Accountability

Community-based monitoring improves transparency and responsiveness. Tools such as:

- **Social audits** of health services.
- **Citizen report cards** to evaluate facility performance.

- **Public hearings** on grievances.

These mechanisms allow citizens to assess the quality of care, report gaps, and advocate for change. The involvement of local governance bodies like Panchayati Raj Institutions strengthens democratic accountability.

14.7 Case Studies and Success Stories

In states like Maharashtra and Tamil Nadu, community participation has led to:

- Improved institutional delivery rates.
- Increased immunization coverage.
- Better sanitation and hygiene practices.
- Reduced maternal and neonatal deaths.

NGOs like SEWA (Self Employed Women's Association) and PRADAN (Professional Assistance for Development Action) have also demonstrated how women-led community models enhance access to care and foster social cohesion.

14.8 Integrating Traditional Knowledge and Practices

Involving local healers and traditional birth attendants (TBAs) in community health dialogues can help bridge the gap between traditional practices and modern medicine. Respecting cultural practices while providing scientific information fosters trust and greater uptake of services.

14.9 Future Priorities

To enhance community participation in MCH:

- Strengthen capacity of VHSNCs and SHGs.
- Include marginalized groups in decision-making.
- Provide adequate funding for community-based monitoring.
- Scale up successful models through cross-learning.
- Institutionalize feedback mechanisms within the health system.

14.10 Conclusion

Community participation transforms passive recipients of care into active stakeholders. By involving people in every stage—from planning to evaluation—health programs become more relevant, responsive, and sustainable. In the context of maternal and child health, community-led models not only improve outcomes but also build social capital, solidarity, and long-term resilience.

CHAPTER FIFTEEN

Insurance and Support for Maternal and Child Health

Financial protection is a critical component of a well-functioning healthcare system. For maternal and child health (MCH), financial barriers can prevent women and families from accessing necessary care, leading to preventable complications and deaths. Insurance schemes and social safety nets serve to mitigate the economic risks associated with pregnancy, childbirth, and child-rearing, particularly for vulnerable and low-income populations.

15.1 Understanding Financial Risk in Maternal Health

Maternal health services, though essential, often involve high out-of-pocket expenses. These include costs for:

- Antenatal and postnatal checkups.
- Institutional deliveries, particularly in private facilities.
- Medicines and diagnostic tests.
- Emergency transport.
- Nutritional supplements and child immunizations.

Such expenses can lead to catastrophic health spending and impoverishment, especially for those without insurance coverage (Xu et al., 2007).

15.2 Role of Health Insurance in MCH

Health insurance helps protect households from financial shocks by covering some or all health-related expenses. In India, several schemes have been introduced with MCH in focus:

- **Janani Suraksha Yojana (JSY)**: A conditional cash transfer program encouraging institutional deliveries among poor pregnant women.
- **Pradhan Mantri Jan Arogya Yojana (PM-JAY)**: Provides secondary and tertiary care hospitalization coverage of ₹5 lakhs per family per year.
- **Employees' State Insurance Scheme (ESIS)**: Offers maternity benefits and healthcare access for registered workers.
- **Ayushman Bharat Health Insurance**: Targets economically disadvantaged populations with comprehensive coverage.

These schemes improve service utilization while reducing out-of-pocket expenditures (Karan, Yip, & Mahal, 2017).

15.3 Conditional Cash Transfers and Maternity Benefits

Conditional cash transfer (CCT) programs aim to incentivize health-seeking behavior through financial rewards:

- **Indira Gandhi Matritva Sahyog Yojana (IGMSY)**: Offers partial wage compensation to pregnant and lactating women.
- **Pradhan Mantri Matru Vandana Yojana (PMMVY)**: Provides ₹5,000 for the first live birth on fulfilling ANC and child immunization milestones.

These programs enhance maternal nutrition, ANC registration, and adherence to health advice.

15.4 Public Distribution and Supplementary Nutrition

- **Integrated Child Development Services (ICDS)** and **Mid-Day Meal Scheme** offer nutritional support to pregnant women and young children.
- **Public Distribution System (PDS)** ensures subsidized food grains, which indirectly support maternal and child nutrition.

These safety nets reduce food insecurity, which is a major determinant of maternal and infant morbidity.

15.5 Community-Based Health Financing Models

In some regions, community financing models have emerged as alternatives to formal insurance:

- **Micro-insurance schemes** managed by SHGs or cooperatives.
- **Mutual aid funds** in tribal or rural areas.
- **Health cooperatives** offering pooled risk-sharing among members.

Such models are context-specific, leveraging community trust and participation to enhance access to care (Dror & Jacquier, 1999).

15.6 Evaluating the Effectiveness of Financial Protection

The impact of financial protection schemes can be assessed using indicators such as:

- Reduction in out-of-pocket spending.
- Increase in institutional deliveries and ANC visits.
- Utilization of insurance benefits.
- Improvement in maternal and neonatal health outcomes.

Independent audits, household surveys, and health system reports are useful in evaluating policy performance.

15.7 Barriers to Financial Protection

Despite several initiatives, challenges persist:

- Low awareness and poor enrollment rates.
- Delays in reimbursement and paperwork.
- Exclusion of informal workers and migrants.
- Gendered access to financial services and insurance literacy.

Policy reforms are needed to make schemes more inclusive, accessible, and efficient.

15.8 Integrating Financial Protection with Universal Health Coverage (UHC)

Achieving UHC requires embedding financial protection into broader health system goals. This includes:

- Expanding primary care services.
- Linking insurance schemes with public health delivery.
- Removing user fees and ensuring free maternal health services.
- Strengthening governance and accountability.

The goal is to ensure that no woman or child is denied care due to inability to pay.

15.9 Future Priorities

- Increase awareness about entitlements and schemes.
- Use digital platforms for enrollment and claim tracking.
- Focus on marginalized groups including urban poor and migrants.
- Strengthen data systems to monitor impact.
- Collaborate with private sector for expanded coverage.

15.10 Conclusion

Financial protection mechanisms like insurance, cash transfers, and safety nets are essential to ensuring equitable access to maternal and child health services. As India progresses toward universal health coverage, focusing on the financial dimension of healthcare—especially for women and children—will be key to reducing inequalities, improving health outcomes, and achieving Sustainable Development Goals.

CHAPTER SIXTEEN

Economic Impact of Maternal and Child Health Outcomes

Maternal and child health (MCH) outcomes have significant economic consequences at both micro and macro levels. The direct and indirect costs associated with poor MCH outcomes impact households, healthcare systems, and the broader economy. This chapter explores how investing in maternal and child health generates long-term economic benefits and how poor outcomes can perpetuate cycles of poverty and underdevelopment.

16.1 Direct Economic Costs of Poor MCH

Poor maternal and child health outcomes result in significant direct costs, including:

- Hospitalization due to complications in pregnancy or childbirth.
- Long-term care for children with birth injuries or developmental disorders.
- Treatment of infections, malnutrition, and other preventable conditions.

These costs are often borne out-of-pocket by families, particularly in low-resource settings, contributing to financial hardship and reduced savings.

16.2 Indirect Economic Costs

Indirect costs include:

- Loss of productivity due to maternal morbidity or mortality.
- Reduced labor force participation of caregivers.
- Educational disruptions for children due to poor health.
- Intergenerational impacts of poor health on cognitive development and earning potential.

These costs affect not only individual households but also reduce economic output and human capital development at the national level.

16.3 Economic Benefits of Investing in MCH

Investments in MCH can yield high returns:

- Improved maternal health enhances women's workforce participation.
- Child health investments improve educational attainment and future productivity.
- Prevention and early intervention reduce healthcare costs over time.

The World Bank and WHO have consistently emphasized the cost-effectiveness of MCH interventions, especially in resource-limited settings.

16.4 MCH and Human Capital Development

Healthy mothers and children are essential for building a productive workforce. Human capital theory suggests that early-life health investments significantly influence future earnings and economic mobility. Countries with strong MCH outcomes tend to have higher economic growth rates.

16.5 Macroeconomic Implications

At the macro level, improved MCH outcomes contribute to:

- Lower fertility and improved demographic transitions.
- Increased female labor participation.
- Reduced healthcare system burden.
- Enhanced national productivity and GDP growth.

Conversely, poor MCH outcomes can lead to a demographic trap, where high fertility and poor health undermine economic progress.

16.6 Economic Models for Evaluating MCH Interventions

Cost-benefit and cost-effectiveness analyses are widely used to evaluate MCH interventions. Models such as DALYs (Disability-Adjusted Life Years) and QALYs (Quality-Adjusted Life Years) help policymakers prioritize investments based on the greatest health and economic returns.

16.7 Long-Term Societal Impacts

Societal impacts of poor MCH include:

- Increased dependency ratios.
- Greater social spending on disability and welfare.
- Inequities in health and income distribution.

These long-term effects underscore the need for sustained investment in MCH services.

16.8 Policy Recommendations

To optimize economic outcomes, policies should:

- Prioritize preventive MCH services.
- Integrate MCH with broader health and social protection systems.
- Support female education and employment.
- Address regional and socio-economic disparities in access to care.

16.9 Conclusion

Maternal and child health is not only a social and moral imperative but also an economic one. Improved MCH outcomes lead to healthier populations, stronger economies, and more equitable societies. Strategic investments in this sector are essential for sustainable development and long-term national prosperity.

CHAPTER SEVENTEEN

Integrating Maternal and Child Health into Economic Policies

Maternal and child health (MCH) lies at the heart of sustainable development. Integrating MCH into economic policy frameworks is vital for achieving equitable growth, social justice, and the Sustainable Development Goals (SDGs). This chapter examines how MCH can be mainstreamed into broader development strategies and the implications for long-term national and global economic prosperity.

17.1 MCH and the Sustainable Development Goals (SDGs)

SDG 3 aims to ensure healthy lives and promote well-being for all at all ages, with specific targets on reducing maternal mortality and ending preventable child deaths. However, MCH is also linked to:

- **SDG 1 (No Poverty):** Reducing healthcare-related impoverishment.
- **SDG 2 (Zero Hunger):** Addressing maternal and child malnutrition.
- **SDG 4 (Quality Education):** Promoting early childhood development.
- **SDG 5 (Gender Equality):** Empowering women through access to reproductive health services.
- **SDG 8 (Decent Work and Economic Growth):** Enabling women's labor force participation.

Thus, MCH is both a standalone goal and a catalyst for progress across multiple SDGs.

17.2 Policy Integration and Intersectoral Collaboration

Effective integration of MCH into national development strategies requires:

- **Intersectoral coordination**: Collaboration between health, education, nutrition, sanitation, and labor ministries.
- **Policy coherence**: Aligning health financing with broader economic and social protection goals.
- **Decentralized planning**: Empowering local governments to tailor MCH services to community needs.
- **Public-private partnerships**: Leveraging resources and innovation from the private sector.

Examples include India's Aspirational Districts Programme, which uses a convergence model to improve health and development indicators.

17.3 Financing MCH through Development Budgets

Governments must prioritize MCH in national budgets:

- Increase domestic health spending as a percentage of GDP.
- Introduce gender-responsive budgeting.
- Channel development aid towards integrated MCH programs.
- Promote social health insurance and community-based financing schemes.

The Abuja Declaration recommends allocating at least 15% of national budgets to health.

17.4 Monitoring and Accountability Frameworks

Robust monitoring systems help track progress and ensure accountability:

- Use of indicators like maternal mortality ratio (MMR), under-five mortality rate (U5MR), and skilled birth attendance.
- Data disaggregation by income, geography, caste, and gender.
- Civil society engagement in budget tracking and social audits.

These tools promote transparency and citizen participation.

17.5 Economic Empowerment of Women through MCH

Improving MCH contributes to women's economic empowerment:

- Healthy women are more likely to participate in education and employment.
- Access to contraception and reproductive health services allows for career planning.
- Reduced caregiving burden enables greater workforce engagement.

Women's economic participation, in turn, drives economic growth and poverty reduction.

17.6 Global Commitments and National Adaptation

International frameworks such as the Global Strategy for Women's, Children's and Adolescents' Health (2016–2030) guide national action. Countries should:

- Align national health plans with global targets.
- Participate in global monitoring platforms.
- Share best practices and innovations.

India's National Health Policy (2017) and Reproductive, Maternal, Newborn, Child, and Adolescent Health (RMNCH+A) strategy align with these global goals.

17.7 Challenges and the Way Forward

Key challenges include:

- Fragmentation of services.
- Inadequate financing and human resources.
- Inequities in access across social and geographic groups.
- Weak data systems and limited use of evidence in policymaking.

Recommendations:

- Promote integrated service delivery.
- Strengthen primary healthcare systems.
- Enhance capacity building and training.
- Institutionalize evidence-based policymaking.

17.8 Conclusion

Mainstreaming maternal and child health into economic policies is essential for sustainable development. It requires a coordinated, multi-sectoral approach that addresses the social determinants of health and promotes gender equity. By investing in MCH, countries can secure healthier populations, empower women, and foster inclusive economic growth.

References

1. Agarwal, S., Labrique, A., & Mehl, G. (2015). Scaling digital health innovations: Lessons from pregnancy and newborn care initiatives in India. *Journal of Global Health, 5*(1), 010301.
2. Bajpai, N., & Goyal, S. (2004). Improving access and efficiency in public health services: Mid-term evaluation of India's National Rural Health Mission. Earth Institute.
3. Baru, R., Acharya, A., Acharya, S., Kumar, A. K. S., & Nagaraj, K. (2010). Inequities in access to health services in India: Caste, class and region. *Economic and Political Weekly, 45*(38), 49–58.
4. Becker, G. S. (1993). *Human capital: A theoretical and empirical analysis, with special reference to education* (3rd ed.). University of Chicago Press.
5. Berman, P., Ahuja, R., & Bhandari, L. (2010). The impoverishing effect of healthcare payments in India: New methodology and findings. *Economic and Political Weekly, 45*(16), 65–71.
6. Bhat, R., Mavalankar, D., Singh, P. V., & Singh, N. (2009). Maternal healthcare financing: Gujarat's Chiranjeevi Scheme and its beneficiaries. *Journal of Health, Population, and Nutrition, 27*(2), 249–258.
7. Bhawra, J., Kirkpatrick, S. I., McCann, W., & Tarasuk, V. (2020). Food insecurity and nutritional risk among Canadian women during pregnancy. *Canadian Journal of Public Health, 111*(5), 717–725.
8. Bhutta, Z. A., Lassi, Z. S., Pariyo, G., & Huicho, L. (2010). Global experience of community health workers for delivery of health-related Millennium Development Goals: A systematic review. *World Health Organization.*
9. Black, R. E., Victora, C. G., Walker, S. P., Bhutta, Z. A., Christian, P., De Onis, M., ... & Uauy, R. (2013). Maternal and child undernutrition and overweight in low-income and middle-income countries. *The Lancet, 382*(9890), 427–451.
10. Bohren, M. A., Hunter, E. C., Munthe-Kaas, H. M., Souza, J. P., Vogel, J. P., & Gülmezoglu, A. M. (2015). Facilitators and barriers to facility-based delivery in low-and middle-income countries: A qualitative evidence synthesis. *Reproductive Health, 11*(1), 71.
11. Bronfenbrenner, U. (1979). *The ecology of human development: Experiments by nature and design.* Harvard University Press.

12. Duflo, E. (2012). Women empowerment and economic development. *Journal of Economic Literature, 50*(4), 1051–1079.

13. Drèze, J., & Goyal, A. (2003). Future of Mid-Day Meals. *Economic and Political Weekly, 38*(44), 4673–4683.

14. Engel, G. L. (1977). The need for a new medical model: A challenge for biomedicine. *Science, 196*(4286), 129–136.

15. Gopichandran, V., Chetlapalli, S. K., & Kumar, R. (2017). Mobile phone-based health education for pregnant women in India. *Journal of Health Communication, 22*(3), 216–223.

16. Grossman, M. (1972). On the concept of health capital and the demand for health. *Journal of Political Economy, 80*(2), 223–255.

17. Gwatkin, D. R., Wagstaff, A., & Yazbeck, A. S. (Eds.). (2007). *Reaching the poor with health, nutrition, and population services: What works, what doesn't, and why.* The World Bank.

18. Halfon, N., & Hochstein, M. (2002). Life course health development: An integrated framework for developing health, policy, and research. *The Milbank Quarterly, 80*(3), 433–479.

19. Hoddinott, J., Alderman, H., Behrman, J. R., Haddad, L., & Horton, S. (2013). The economic rationale for investing in stunting reduction. *Maternal & Child Nutrition, 9*(S2), 69–82.

20. International Institute for Population Sciences (IIPS) & ICF. (2021). *National Family Health Survey (NFHS-5), 2019–21: India.* Mumbai: IIPS.

21. International Institute for Population Sciences (IIPS) & Macro International. (1995). *National Family Health Survey (NFHS-1), 1992–93: India.* Mumbai: IIPS.

22. Jain, A., & Raza, N. (2020). Artificial Intelligence in maternal and child health: Opportunities and challenges in India. *Indian Journal of Public Health, 64*(3), 228–232.

23. Jamison, D. T., Summers, L. H., Alleyne, G., Arrow, K. J., Berkley, S., Binagwaho, A., ... & Yamey, G. (2013). Global health 2035: A world converging within a generation. *The Lancet, 382*(9908), 1898–1955.

24. Karan, A., Selvaraj, S., & Mahal, A. (2017). Moving to universal coverage? Trends in the burden of out-of-pocket payments for health care across social groups in India, 1999–2000 to 2011–12. *PloS One, 9*(8), e105162.

25. Karan, A., Yip, W., & Mahal, A. (2017). Extending health insurance to the poor in India: An impact evaluation of Rashtriya Swasthya Bima Yojana on out-of-pocket spending for healthcare. *Social Science & Medicine, 181*, 83–92.

26. Lim, S. S., Dandona, L., Hoisington, J. A., James, S. L., Hogan, M. C., & Gakidou, E. (2010). India's Janani Suraksha Yojana, a conditional cash transfer programme to increase births in health facilities: An impact evaluation. *The Lancet, 375*(9730), 2009–2023.

27. Ministry of Health and Family Welfare (MoHFW). (2013). *Janani Shishu Suraksha Karyakram: Operational Guidelines.*

28. Ministry of Health and Family Welfare (MoHFW). (2021). *Mission Indradhanush: Strategy and operational guidelines.*

29. Ministry of Health and Family Welfare (MoHFW). (2021). *National Health Mission Status Report.*

30. Ministry of Health and Family Welfare (MoHFW). (2018). *National Health Mission: Framework for Implementation.*

31. Ministry of Health and Family Welfare. (2021). *Rural Health Statistics 2020–21.*

32. Ministry of Women and Child Development (MoWCD). (2018). *Pradhan Mantri Matru Vandana Yojana Guidelines.*

33. Ministry of Women and Child Development. (2021). *Annual Report 2020–21.*

34. National Family Health Survey. (2021). *NFHS-5 Fact Sheets.* International Institute for Population Sciences (IIPS).

35. National Health Accounts. (2021). *Estimates for India (2017–18).* Ministry of Health and Family Welfare.

36. National Health Accounts. (2022). *Estimates for India (2018–19).* Ministry of Health and Family Welfare.

37. National Health Systems Resource Centre. (2020). *National Health Resource Repository.*

38. NITI Aayog. (2020). *Healthy States, Progressive India: Report on the Ranks of States and Union Territories.*

39. NITI Aayog. (2020). *Strategy for New India @75.*

40. Patel, V., Parikh, R., Nandraj, S., Balasubramaniam, P., Narayan, K., Paul, V. K., ... & Reddy, K. S. (2015). Assuring health coverage for all in India. *The Lancet, 386*(10011), 2422–2435.

41. Registrar General of India. (2022). *Sample Registration System: Special Bulletin on Maternal Mortality in India 2018–20.*

42. Rifkin, S. B. (2009). Lessons from community participation in health programmes: A review of the post-Alma-Ata experience. *International Journal of Health Planning and Management, 24*(1), 23–44.

43. Rao, K. D., Petrosyan, V., Araujo, E. C., & McIntyre, D. (2012). Progress

towards universal health coverage in BRICS: Translating economic growth into better health. *Bulletin of the World Health Organization, 90*(7), 486–490.

44. Rao, K. D., Ramani, S., Muraleedharan, V. R., & Gilson, L. (2011). Health systems financing and equity: Lessons from India. *Social Science & Medicine, 72*(4), 560–567.

45. Saha, S. (2017). Microfinance and women's empowerment: An empirical analysis using panel data from India. *World Development, 90,* 269–281.

46. Sample Registration System. (2022). *Maternal mortality in India: 2018–20.* Office of the Registrar General.

47. Sen, G., & Östlin, P. (2008). Gender inequity in health: Why it exists and how we can change it. *Global Public Health, 3*(S1), 1–12.

48. Singh, P., Ravi, S., & Bansal, S. (2018). Digital health: A policy perspective. *Brookings India Impact Series, October.*

49. Tangcharoensathien, V., Patcharanarumol, W., Ir, P., Aljunid, S. M., Mukti, A. G., Akkhavong, K., ... & Mills, A. (2018). Health-financing reforms in southeast Asia: Challenges in achieving universal coverage. *The Lancet, 377*(9768), 863–873.

50. UNFPA India. (2021). *Impact of COVID-19 on sexual and reproductive health in India: Evidence and recommendations.*

51. UNICEF. (2001). *A human rights-based approach to programming for children and women: What is it, and how to do it.* New York: UNICEF.

52. UNICEF. (2014). *RMNCH+A Strategy.* Retrieved from https://www.unicef.org/india/reports/rmncha-strategy

53. UNICEF. (2018). *Adolescents, Diets and Nutrition: Growing Well in a Changing World.* New York: UNICEF.

54. UNICEF. (2019). *A review of Janani Shishu Suraksha Karyakram and its impact on out-of-pocket expenditure and maternal and neonatal health.* UNICEF India.

55. UNICEF. (2019). *Kilkari and Mobile Academy: Reaching India's mothers and ASHAs with health information.* New Delhi: UNICEF India.

56. UNICEF. (2023). *Child mortality estimates.* Retrieved from https://data.unicef.org/topic/child-survival/under-five-mortality/

57. World Bank. (2019). *Poverty and shared prosperity 2018: Piecing together the poverty puzzle.* World Bank Publications.

58. World Health Organization. (2008). *Closing the gap in a generation: Health equity through action on the social determinants of health.* Final Report of the Commission on Social Determinants of Health.

59. World Health Organization. (2010). *Health systems financing: The path to universal coverage.* Geneva: WHO.
60. World Health Organization. (2015). *Global investment framework for women's and children's health.*
61. World Health Organization. (2016). *Health workforce requirements for universal health coverage and the Sustainable Development Goals.*
62. World Health Organization (WHO). (2016). *Standards for improving quality of maternal and newborn care in health facilities.* Geneva: WHO.
63. Xu, K., Evans, D. B., Kawabata, K., Zeramdini, R., Klavus, J., & Murray, C. J. (2003). Household catastrophic health expenditure: A multicountry analysis. *The Lancet, 362*(9378), 111–117.

Glossary

- **Antenatal Care (ANC):** Medical and preventive healthcare services provided to pregnant women to ensure a healthy pregnancy and safe delivery.
- **Child Mortality Rate:** The number of deaths of children under five years of age per 1,000 live births.
- **Cost-Effectiveness Analysis (CEA):** A method to assess the gains in health relative to the costs of different health interventions.
- **DALY (Disability-Adjusted Life Year):** A measure that combines years of life lost due to premature death and years lived with disability to assess the overall disease burden.
- **Gender-Responsive Budgeting:** The process of planning and allocating national or local budgets that take into account the different needs and contributions of women and men.
- **Human Capital:** The skills, knowledge, and experience possessed by an individual or population, viewed in terms of their value or cost to an organization or country.
- **Intergenerational Impact:** The effect of one generation's health or socioeconomic status on the well-being of future generations.
- **Maternal Mortality Ratio (MMR):** The number of maternal deaths per 100,000 live births in a given time period.
- **MCH (Maternal and Child Health):** A field of public health focused on improving the health and well-being of mothers, infants, and children.
- **Primary Healthcare:** Essential health care based on scientifically sound methods, made universally accessible to individuals and families in the community.
- **Reproductive Health:** A state of physical, mental, and social well-being in all matters relating to the reproductive system.
- **RMNCH+A (Reproductive, Maternal, Newborn, Child, and Adolescent Health):** An integrated strategy addressing health care across different life stages.
- **SDGs (Sustainable Development Goals):** A collection of 17 global goals set by the United Nations to achieve a better and more sustainable future for all.
- **Under-Five Mortality Rate (U5MR):** The probability that a child born

in a specific year or period will die before reaching the age of five, expressed per 1,000 live births.
- **Universal Health Coverage (UHC):** Ensuring that all individuals and communities receive the health services they need without suffering financial hardship.

Index

www.ingramcontent.com/pod-product-compliance
Lightning Source LLC
Chambersburg PA
CBHW040826120726
48005CB00012B/1518